SCIENCE FILES

materials

METALS

Please visit our web site at: www.garethstevens.com
For a free color catalog describing Gareth Stevens Publishing's
list of high-quality books and multimedia programs,
call 1-800-542-2595 or fax your request to (414) 332-3567.

Library of Congress Cataloging-in-Publication Data

Parker, Steve.
    Metals / by Steve Parker. — North American ed.
      p. cm. — (Science files. Materials)
    Includes bibliographical references and index.
    Summary: Discusses how metals are created, extracted, and worked, and looks at
the uses of metal in the past, present, and future, including artificially produced metal
and metal from outer space.
    ISBN 0-8368-3083-0 (lib. bdg.)
    1. Metals—Juvenile literature. [1. Metals.] I. Title.
TN148.P344   2002
669—dc21   2001054228

This North American edition first published in 2002 by
Gareth Stevens Publishing
A World Almanac Education Group Company
330 West Olive Street, Suite 100
Milwaukee, WI 53212 USA

Original edition © 2001 by David West Children's Books. First published in Great Britain
in 2001 by Heinemann Library, Halley Court, Jordan Hill, Oxford OX2 8EJ, a division of Reed
Educational and Professional Publishing Limited. This U.S. edition © 2002 by Gareth Stevens, Inc.
Additional end matter © 2002 by Gareth Stevens, Inc.

David West Editor: James Pickering
David West Designers: Rob Shone, Fiona Thorne, David West
Picture Research: Carrie Haines
Gareth Stevens Editor: Alan Wachtel
Gareth Stevens Designer and Cover Design: Katherine A. Goedheer

Photo Credits:
Abbreviations: (t) top, (m) middle, (b) bottom, (l) left, (r) right

AKG London: 15br.
Allsport: 27bl.
The Art Archive: British Library (24bl); Deir-ez-Zor Museum, Syria/Dagli Orti (19br); Eileen
Tweedy/London Museum (7br, 11br).
Robert Harding Picture Library: S. Bavister (22tr); Robert Frerck (5tr); Jeff Greenberg@uno.com
(20bl); Peter Scholey (10bl); Bildagentur Schuster/Schiller (23bl, 23t, 24br, 26r); Maximilian Stock Ltd.
(19ml); A.C. Waltham (4tr, 8tr); Earl Young (18bl); 9tl, 17tl, 18-19t, 19m, 21br.
Hulton-Archive: 26b.
Science Photo Library: Vaughan Fleming (27tr); Astrid and Hanns-Frieder Michler (14tr); Dr. Morley
Read (cover [tr], 24tr); Rosenfeld Images Ltd. (4-5b, 10tr); Peter Thorne/Johnson Matthey (25br); U.S.
Dept. of Energy (8bl); 6-7b, 28br.
The Stock Market: H. Halberstadt (14m, 27mr).

Printed in the United States of America

1 2 3 4 5 6 7 8 9 06 05 04 03 02

SCIENCE FILES

materials

METALS

Steve Parker

Gareth Stevens Publishing

A WORLD ALMANAC EDUCATION GROUP COMPANY

CONTENTS

Most metals come from Earth's rocks. The rocks that are rich in metals are known as ores. They are dug up, or mined. These rocks are being mined because they contain the metal copper.

Ore rock is usually mixed with various chemicals and heated in a furnace. The ore melts and the pure metal flows out.

INTRODUCTION

How is a golden crown similar to a car, a jumbo jet, a thumbtack, and the girders of a skyscraper? They are all made of metals. Most metals are hard, strong, shiny, and long-lasting. Dozens of different metals are vital in our modern world. Some, such as iron and aluminum, are used in huge amounts. Others, such as tungsten and palladium, are used in tiny quantities. We obtain metals from Earth's rocks. The supply of metal-containing rocks is limited, and getting metals out of the rocks uses huge amounts of energy. For this reason, it is vital to conserve and recycle metals for the future.

Rare metals, such as the gold in this statue, are valued for their beauty.

Some metals are common and valued for practical uses. These car bodies are made from steel, an alloy of iron and carbon.

WORLD OF METALS

Metals such as gold, silver, or copper are very rarely found lying on the ground as nuggets, or almost-pure lumps. Most of Earth's metals are joined or combined with various other substances and spread thinly through the planet's rocks.

METAL ORES

A rock that is rich in a certain metal is known as an ore. Scientists called geologists test samples of rocks from certain places to see if they are ores and to find out which metals they contain. Then they decide whether more rocks that come from the same place as the samples should be mined for the metals in them.

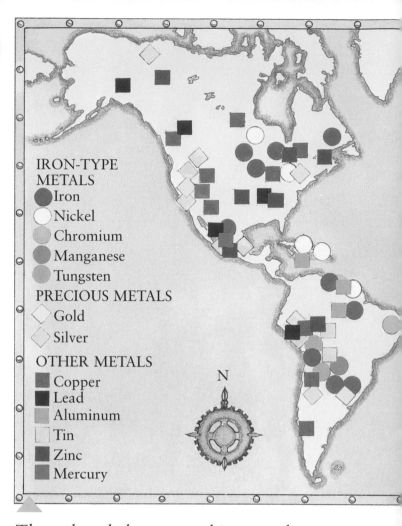

IRON-TYPE METALS
- Iron
- Nickel
- Chromium
- Manganese
- Tungsten

PRECIOUS METALS
- Gold
- Silver

OTHER METALS
- Copper
- Lead
- Aluminum
- Tin
- Zinc
- Mercury

N

The colored shapes on this map show which metals are found around the world. But not all places have enough metal to make them worth mining. Many remote places are still being explored for metals.

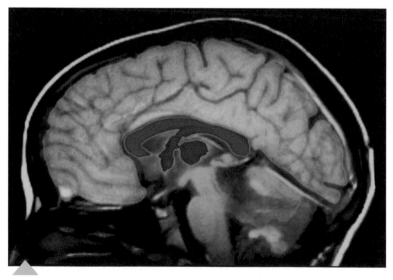

Sodium, potassium, and calcium are metallic elements that the human body needs to be healthy. This image is a scan of the brain.

6

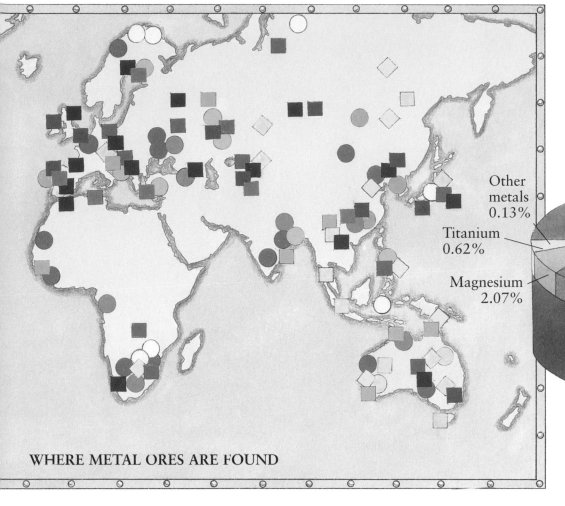

WHERE METAL ORES ARE FOUND

Only about 25% (one-quarter) of Earth's rocky outer layer, or crust, is made of metals.

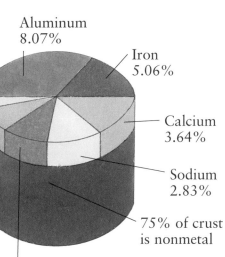

Other metals 0.13%

Aluminum 8.07%

Iron 5.06%

Titanium 0.62%

Calcium 3.64%

Magnesium 2.07%

Sodium 2.83%

75% of crust is nonmetal

Potassium 2.58%

LOOKING FOR METAL ORES

Geologists use many methods to search, or prospect, for rocks rich in metals. Photographs taken by satellites in space show how some rocks form in certain shapes or layers. These shapes suggest that the rocks contain metals. Also, large clumps of ores affect Earth's gravity or natural magnetism. Sensitive detectors measure how these forces vary and show where metals may be hidden.

Many tests are needed to check rocks for metals. This looks like gold, but it is really only a worthless rock called "fool's gold."

FACTS FROM THE PAST

Certain metals were so important to people in ancient times that periods of history are named after them. After the Stone Age, the first main "metal age" was the Bronze Age. It began over 5,000 years ago in the region known today as the Middle East.

A bronze spear tip from Europe

7

MINING METALS

The rocks called ores, which are rich in metals, are mined from the ground in many ways. Soft ores at Earth's surface can be scooped up. Other ores are dug from tunnels hundreds of feet below the surface using powerful drills, cutters, and explosives such as dynamite.

ORES AT THE SURFACE

Digging up ores at the surface is called strip-mining. Several metals, including copper, aluminum, and iron, are strip-mined. The ore is loosened and broken up by dynamite blasts or drills and loaded onto huge trucks by excavator machines that can lift tens of tons in one bucket load.

The USA's Bingham Canyon copper mine is the world's largest man-made hole.

HOW ORES FORM

Ores form in many ways. Magma (1) — rock so hot it is molten — lies deep underground. Rocks form from cooling magma, leaving behind a mixture of hot water and metal particles. This mix runs into nearby rocks (2) and the metals are deposited. Rainwater seeps into the ground, carrying the metals to spongy parts of rock (3). Metals may also collect in the volcano's lava (4). Rivers wash metals out of rocks and send them to settle in lakes and seas (5), or water far below the ocean floor can carry metals up into cracks (6) or into springs in the seabed (7).

Geologists use tube-shaped drills to take out "rods" of rock called cores. Cores are tested to see if they contain metals.

Mining for iron ore in Sweden's Kiruna region takes place deep underground in very hot and humid conditions.

ORES DEEP UNDERGROUND

Many ores are found as narrow layers of rock, called veins or seams. Mining the ore is easier at the surface. As the layer runs deeper, shafts and tunnels must be dug to reach it. The ore is often broken up by drills. But sometimes holes are drilled in the rock for sticks of explosives. Then everyone moves through tunnels to a safe distance, and BANG!

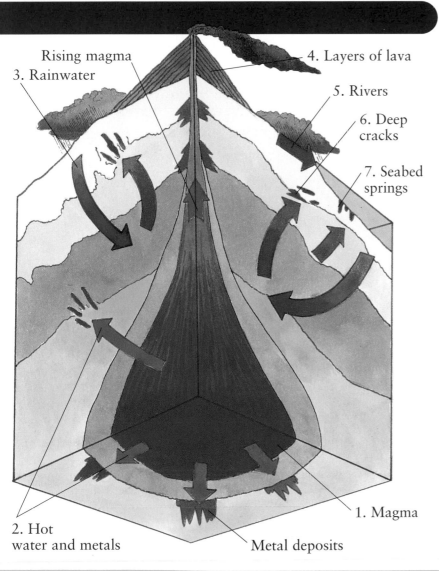

Rising magma
3. Rainwater
4. Layers of lava
5. Rivers
6. Deep cracks
7. Seabed springs
1. Magma
2. Hot water and metals
Metal deposits

Crust
Mantle
Outer core
Inner core

IDEAS FOR THE FUTURE

Earth's core is made of metals — mostly iron, with some nickel. It has enough of these metals to supply our industries almost forever. But reaching the core means drilling through Earth's middle layer, the mantle. At 1,800 miles (2,900 km) thick, that would take almost forever!

9

FROM ORE TO IRON

Although iron is the most widely used metal in the world, very little of it is used in the form of pure iron. Most iron is added to other substances, especially carbon, to make steel.

A HUGE INDUSTRY

Iron is so important that mining its ores and refining them in order to extract, or get out, the metal is one of the world's biggest industries. In rocks, iron is usually found in other forms because it combines with other substances, such as oxygen and sulfur. When iron combines with oxygen, the mixture is called iron oxide. When it mixes with sulfur, the mixture is called iron sulfide.

THE BLAST FURNACE

Iron ore is ground and mixed with coke and limestone. These raw materials pour into the blast furnace, a tower over 98 feet (30 meters) tall. The coke burns at over 1,830° Fahrenheit (1,000° Celsius) to melt the ore. Pig iron is used to make steel, while the impurities collect as slag.

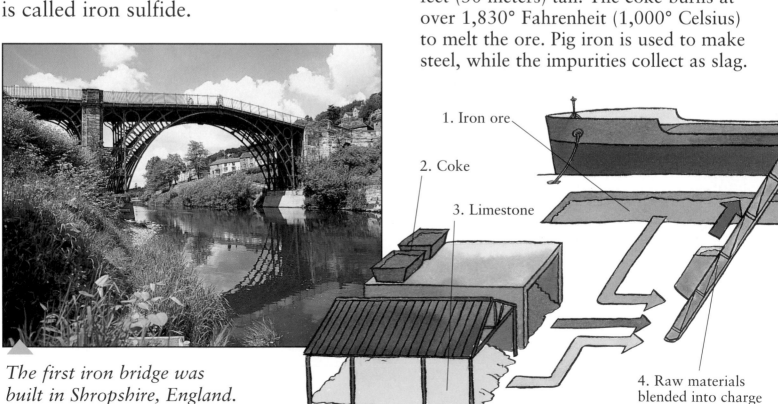

1. Iron ore

2. Coke

3. Limestone

4. Raw materials blended into charge

The first iron bridge was built in Shropshire, England.

As iron ore melts, the iron forms a separate layer. Workers take samples to test the melted metal for purity. They wear special clothes to protect them against the 2,730° F (1,500° C) temperature.

SMELTING

Like most metals, iron is extracted by the basic process of smelting, or heating, its ores. Smelting happens in a giant oven called the blast furnace. The fuel burned to heat the ore is coke. Coke contains substances that combine with the oxygen, sulfur, and other chemicals that were part of the ore. Limestone soaks up, or absorbs, these substances. The smelting process allows the iron to become free and fairly pure.

5. Charge poured in

6. Gases are led to heat exchangers

10. Slag drawn off

7. Air preheated in exchanger

9. Pig iron drawn off for steelworks

8. Preheated air blasts into furnace

FACTS FROM THE PAST

The Iron Age began at different times in different regions. About 3,200 years ago, the Hittites of Anatolia (now Turkey) first smelted ores and made fairly pure iron. About 2,800 years ago, these methods spread through Europe. Shaping iron by forging became common about 2,500 years ago.

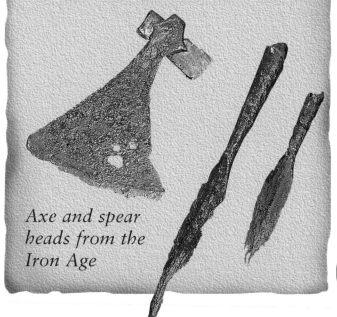

Axe and spear heads from the Iron Age

EXTRACTING METALS

Most metals are extracted from their ores by smelting, or heating (*see page 11*). This does not always produce very pure metal, however, so many metals are also refined, or made more pure.

Aluminum is very light, fairly soft, and easily bent. Millions of cans are made from aluminum every day.

Because copper conducts, or carries, electricity well, it is used for electrical cables and wires.

COPPER

Copper is obtained in two stages. First, its ores arc crushed, mixed with water and chemicals, filtered, and smelted at 2,730° F (1,500° C) with blasts of air and chemicals called fluxes. The result is copper that is 98–99% pure. The next stage is refining by electrolysis (see "Aluminum from Its Ore," *page 13*), which increases its purity to almost 100%.

A worker tests nickel, which is made into coins.

NICKEL

The very hard, shiny metal called nickel does not melt until its temperature is 2,650° F (1,455° C). So nickel ores must be heated much hotter than most other metal ores.

12

Aluminum's main ore is bauxite, which is processed into crystals called alumina (aluminum oxide). These are mixed with cryolite and heated to 1,800° F (980° C) in reduction pots. In a process called electrolysis, a huge amount of electricity — about enough to power a whole city — is passed through the mix, making the pure aluminum separate from the oxygen.

In the reduction pots, alumina is separated into oxygen and pure, molten aluminum.

▼

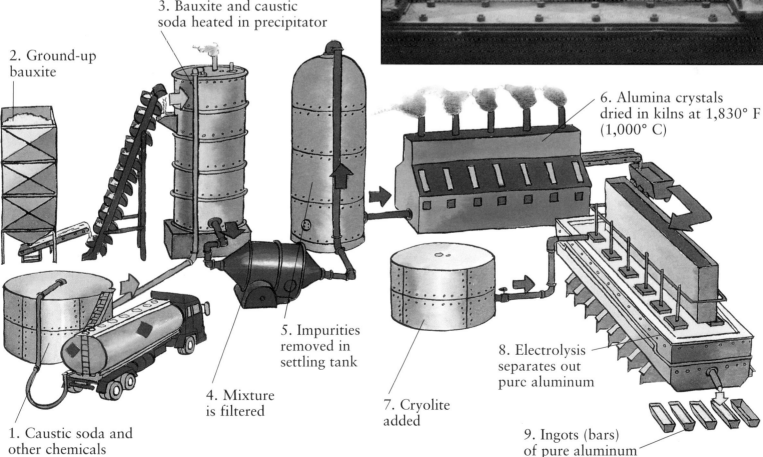

3. Bauxite and caustic soda heated in precipitator

2. Ground-up bauxite

6. Alumina crystals dried in kilns at 1,830° F (1,000° C)

5. Impurities removed in settling tank

8. Electrolysis separates out pure aluminum

4. Mixture is filtered

7. Cryolite added

1. Caustic soda and other chemicals

9. Ingots (bars) of pure aluminum

MAKING ALLOYS

Many metals, after being extracted from their ores and refined to make them more pure, are then added to other substances. Mixing metals with other substances can make the metals stronger, more flexible, or resistant to corrosion and aging.

MANY MIXES

A metal that is carefully mixed or blended with another substance is called an alloy. The other material may be a nonmetal — like carbon, for example — or another metal.

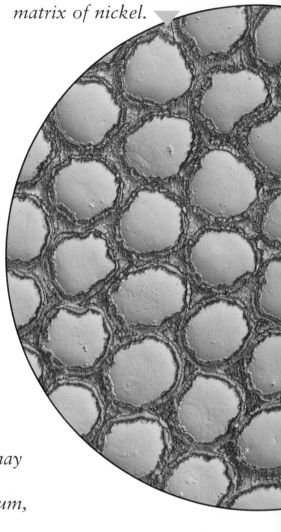

In this closeup of a nickel-silver alloy, micro-blobs of silver are held in a sheet or matrix of nickel.

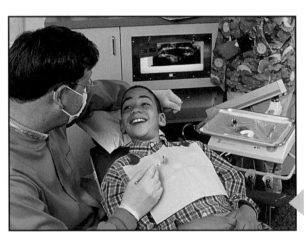

A "gold" dental filling may be an alloy of the metals chromium, cobalt, titanium, and molybdenum.

ALLOYS OF COPPER

Copper is used to make alloys that are easy to shape and able to resist corrosion. The amounts of metal are carefully controlled. Brass that contains about one-fifth zinc is yellow-orange and can be shaped when cold. Brass with almost one-half zinc is whitish and must be shaped hot.

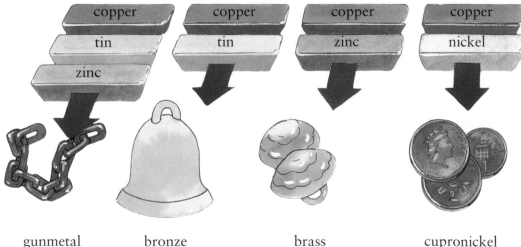

copper	copper	copper	copper
tin	tin	zinc	nickel
zinc			
gunmetal	bronze	brass	cupronickel

14

NEW ALLOYS

Some types of new alloys are called superplastic alloys. Like elastic, they can stretch to twice their length, but these alloys stay very hard and strong. Other types of alloys are known as superconductors. These alloys carry electricity almost perfectly.

Earphones contain tiny but powerful magnets of cobalt-samarium alloy. Without this alloy, the earphones would be huge!

"Silver" and "copper" coins are not pure metals. They are made of alloys, such as silvery, long-lasting cupronickel.

FACTS FROM THE PAST

Alloys of copper, such as bronze, were known long ago — perhaps because copper often occurs in ores with other metals, so alloys formed naturally as the ore was smelted. One poisonous metal-like substance in copper ore is arsenic. In the past, people purifying copper died from exposure to arsenic without knowing the cause.

A bronze helmet from Roman times

THE STEELWORKS

Alloys are metals blended, or mixed, with other substances. When the most often used metal, iron, is mixed with carbon, the result is the world's most widespread alloy — steel.

LOTS OF STEELS

There are thousands of kinds of steel. Each is based on iron and varying amounts of carbon, plus other metals and substances. Standard carbon, or plate, steel is iron with up to one-fiftieth carbon. Plate steel is used in the mass production of items such as car and truck bodies and the outsides of washing machines. Many "tin" cans are made from plate steel that has been coated with a thin layer of tin to stop the steel from rusting or corroding.

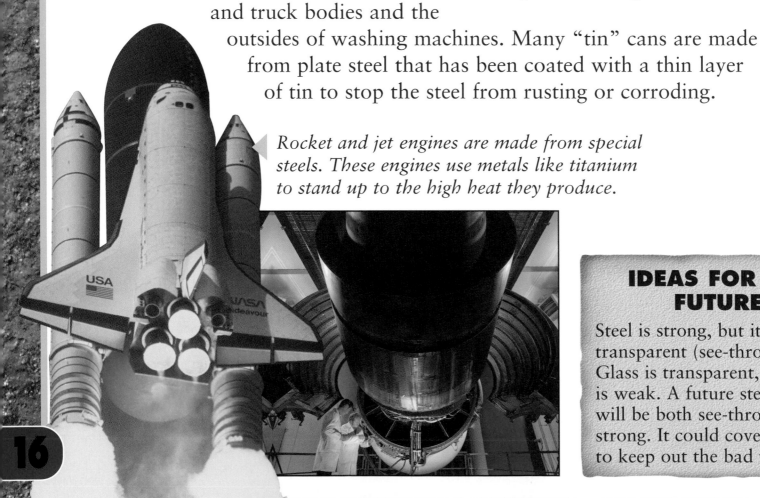

The girders and beams for the frame of a skyscraper are made from steel that is very strong, stiff, and able to bear great weight. This is high-tensile steel.

Rocket and jet engines are made from special steels. These engines use metals like titanium to stand up to the high heat they produce.

IDEAS FOR THE FUTURE

Steel is strong, but it is not transparent (see-through). Glass is transparent, but it is weak. A future steel alloy will be both see-through and strong. It could cover cities to keep out the bad weather.

In the basic process of making pig iron into steel, oxygen is blasted at high pressure for about twenty minutes over melted pig iron in the bottom of a furnace. The oxygen changes the amount of carbon in the iron. The resulting steel is poured out as a huge blob at a temperature of 2,960° F (1,625° C).

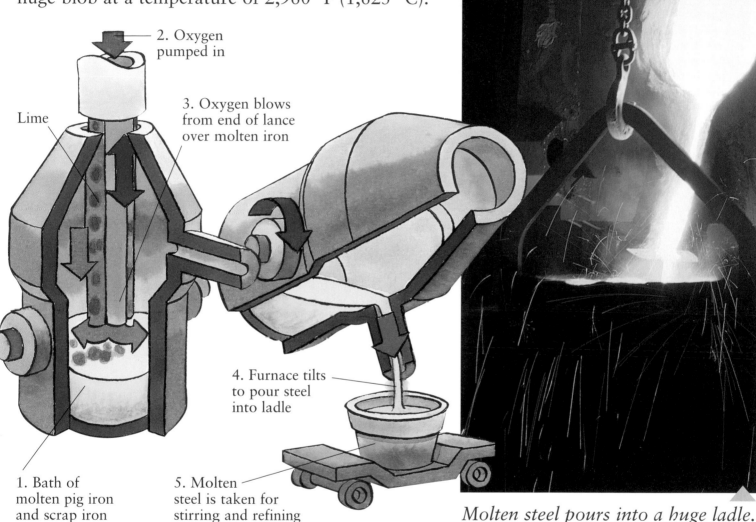

2. Oxygen pumped in

3. Oxygen blows from end of lance over molten iron

Lime

4. Furnace tilts to pour steel into ladle

1. Bath of molten pig iron and scrap iron

5. Molten steel is taken for stirring and refining

Molten steel pours into a huge ladle.

City dome of "Stlass" (transparent steel)

STAINLESS STEELS

One important group of steel alloys is stainless steels. These have added amounts of the shiny metal chromium to make them very hard, smooth, and able to resist scratches, stains, and corrosion. Stainless steels are used for cutlery, sinks, and industrial containers.

SHAPING METALS

Metals seem so hard and strong that they are impossible to bend, squeeze, and mold into certain shapes. Actually, there are many ways of shaping metals — usually with powerful industrial machinery made of even stronger metals.

A molten rod of titanium is drawn, or pulled, through narrowing holes until it is the required thickness.

CHOOSING THE METAL

Each kind of metal has its own special features that make it suitable for shaping in a certain way. For example, copper is very ductile, meaning it can be pulled, or drawn, into long, thin objects such as wires and tubes. Gold and silver are also ductile. They are malleable, too, which means they can be pressed or hammered into very thin sheets, even when cold.

SHAPING HOT METALS

Most metals are shaped as they come out of the furnace where they are made. They can be squeezed into thin sheets by rollers, hammered at the forge, squirted or pulled (drawn) through narrow holes, or cast in hollow molds to cool and solidify.

Molten metal is cast in a mold of sand to harden and cool. The sand will be crumbled and reused.

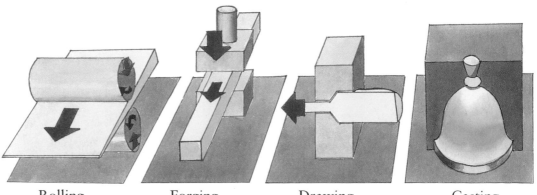

Rolling　　　Forging　　　Drawing　　　Casting

TEMPERING AND TIPPING

Even after a metal object is shaped, it can be altered in various ways. In tempering, the object is heated to a certain temperature, then suddenly "quenched," or cooled, by plunging it into water or oil. Tempering is used especially for steel alloys and makes them harder and stronger. For even greater toughness, another metal may be added. Saw blades and drill bits are usually made of tempered steel, but their tips and edges may be made of a metal that is even more durable than tempered steel — tungsten.

Parts of engines must be machined to the exact size needed for them to fit together.

Items such as can lids and bottle tops are stamped from sheets. The leftover parts of the sheets are melted and recycled.

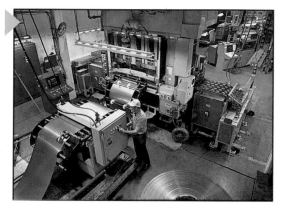

SHAPING COLD METALS

Softer metals, such as aluminum, tin, and mild steel, are shaped while cold. Machining carves metal using grinders and burrs. A lump of metal can be extruded to form a long shape. Presses bend and squeeze with great power. Stamps chop out shapes from sheets.

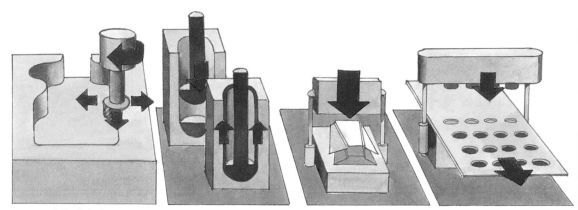

Machining   Extruding   Pressing   Stamping

FACTS FROM THE PAST

Copper was mined and hammered into shape more than 7,000 years ago. It was too soft to make strong, sharp blades and edges, however, leading to the use of its alloy, bronze. *Copper statuette*

19

CUTS AND JOINTS

We cut some materials, such as paper, with scissors or other blades. We also join paper with various materials, such as tape or glue. We can cut and join metals in many different ways, too. But the tools we use are much stronger and more powerful.

CUTTING

Metals like steel are hard. Other substances, however, are even harder. Metals like tungsten and mineral substances like silicon carbide or diamond are so hard that they can cut through most metals by sawing or grinding. High heat from a furnace, blowtorch, or laser beam softens metals so they can be cut more easily. Sometimes the heat even burns right through the metal.

Cutting and welding metal makes sparks fly, so it is vital to wear protective gear.

A powerful laser beam can cut metal with heat. Its narrow beam melts only a small patch of metal, so it is a very accurate cutting tool.

JOINED BY HEAT AND PRESSURE

Friction welding rubs together two metal items until they become so hot that they join together. Very hot burning gases (metal inert gases, or MIG) or an electrical spark, or arc, also weld metal parts together. The heat from

Friction weld   MIG weld   Arc weld

Rivets are like very short nails with their ends hammered over, almost flat.

JOINING

If metal is heated enough, it starts to melt. When two almost-melted metal edges flow together and then cool, the result is a very strong joint called a weld. Metal parts can also be joined by glue, solder, bolts, or rivets.

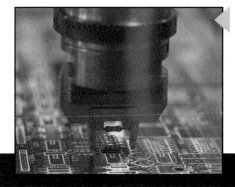

Solder, which melts at about 390° F (200° C), is a soft alloy used like glue to join delicate electrical parts.

a powerful laser beam can melt the edges of metal parts to a jelly so that they flow together and cool to form a joint. Sudden, high pressure from explosives or hammer blows when forging heated metal can have the same joining effect.

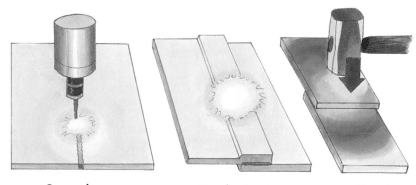

Laser beam   Explosive impact   Forging

IDEAS FOR THE FUTURE

Glues can join most substances strongly. But even super-glues cannot stick certain metals together. Perhaps a new glue will melt the edges of metal parts so they weld. Then we can stick together car parts at home!

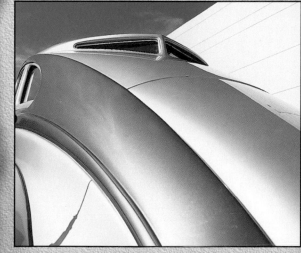

Could future kit cars be glued?

INDUSTRIAL METALS

Many metals are commonly used in factories. Chief among these metals is iron, which is used primarily in the form of its alloy, steel. Other common industrial metals are aluminum, tin, copper, zinc, lead, and chromium.

LIGHT BUT STRONG

Aluminum is very light but fairly strong. Unlike iron and steel, it does not rust, and therefore it is widely used for all kinds of factory-made objects, including ladders, high-power electrical cables, jumbo jets, and pots and pans.

Fireworks contain metals that burn fast and bright and give off colored sparks. Sodium burns yellow, strontium burns red, and barium burns green, while copper and cobalt burn blue.

Most vehicle bodies are made from steel parts. These are inexpensive, light, strong, and easy to cut out, press into large curved shapes, and weld together. They must be protected, however, or they will rust.

Iron is used for more than making huge objects. A thin coating of tiny iron-based particles on video and cassette tapes stores images and sounds as patches of magnetism.

ANTICORROSION

Iron and steel tend to corrode — they become soft, weak, and covered with rust. To protect steel objects against corrosion, they are often covered with a very thin layer of another metal, such as zinc, tin, and chromium, all of which resist corrosion. One method of applying these metals is to melt the anticorrosion metal in a bath and dip the steel object into it. Another method is electroplating (*see below*). Items covered with hard, shiny chromium by this method are said to be "chrome plated."

ELECTROPLATING

Anti-corrosion zinc plating

In electroplating, electricity is passed through liquid between two terminals, positive and negative. The positive terminal is made of the metal that makes the covering layer, or plating. Tiny particles of the metal, called ions, detach from the terminal into the liquid. The electricity carries them to the negative terminal, which is made of the item that receives the plating. The ions of metal stick firmly to it, covering it with a layer of even thickness.

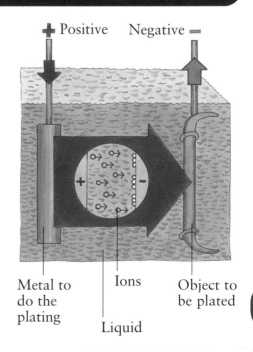

+ Positive   Negative —

Metal to do the plating

Ions

Liquid

Object to be plated

23

PRECIOUS METALS

Silver and gold are very good carriers of electricity. They are used for high-quality electrical wires, switches, and contacts.

Gold! Silver! Some metals have been desired through the ages. People search for years, travel long distances, endure great hardship, sometimes even kill for them. Why?

WHY METALS ARE PRECIOUS

Gold, silver, platinum, and similar metals are precious for several reasons. They have beautiful, glowing colors. They are shiny and long-lasting. They can be hammered and "worked" into tiny, delicate shapes such as rings, necklaces, and bracelets. They are also quite rare, taking much effort to find in rocks and other natural sources and to purify. Owning these metals can be a symbol of wealth and power.

FACTS FROM THE PAST

Long ago, alchemists believed that a magic substance called the "philosopher's stone" could turn ordinary metals into pure gold. Such a substance has never been found.

Alchemists search for gold

Chemicals containing silver are used in camera film. The chemicals change color when light shines on them to produce a picture on the film.

24

Tiny pieces of pure gold can be found naturally, especially in river mud.

Gold can be obtained from slag — the material left over after refining ores of other metals. The slag heap is washed by a high-pressure hose. Pieces containing gold settle to the bottom. They are mixed with the chemical sodium cyanide, which takes up the gold and leaves other substances behind. Then zinc is added to join with the cyanide, freeing the gold particles. These are pressed, dried, and heated to remove water and other impurities and then smelted in a furnace to yield gold.

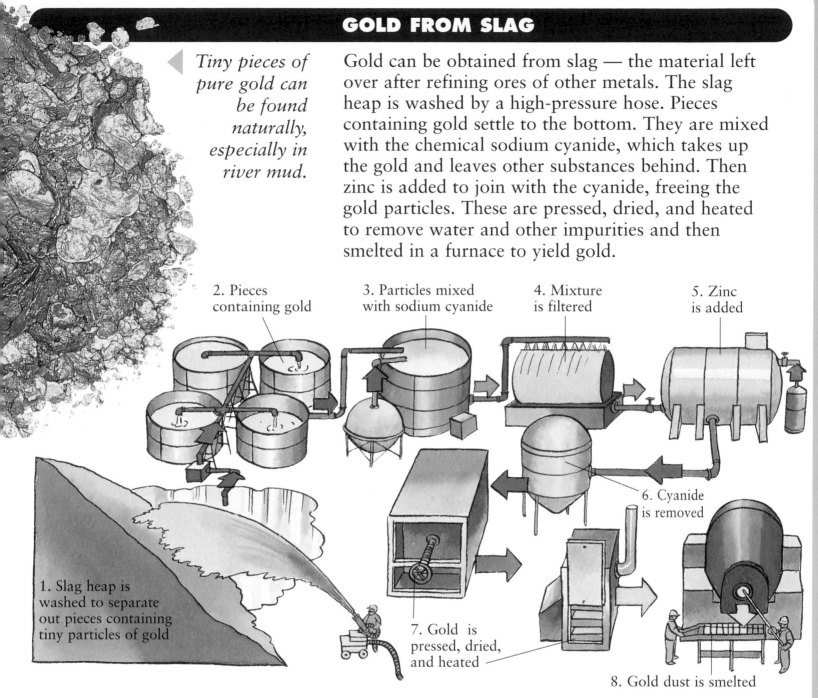

2. Pieces containing gold

3. Particles mixed with sodium cyanide

4. Mixture is filtered

5. Zinc is added

6. Cyanide is removed

1. Slag heap is washed to separate out pieces containing tiny particles of gold

7. Gold is pressed, dried, and heated

8. Gold dust is smelted

METAL MONEY

Gold and silver were once used for coins. Today, their place has been taken by less expensive, more durable alloys. But gold and silver bars, or ingots, are still used by banks in special cases.

Gold ingots ▶

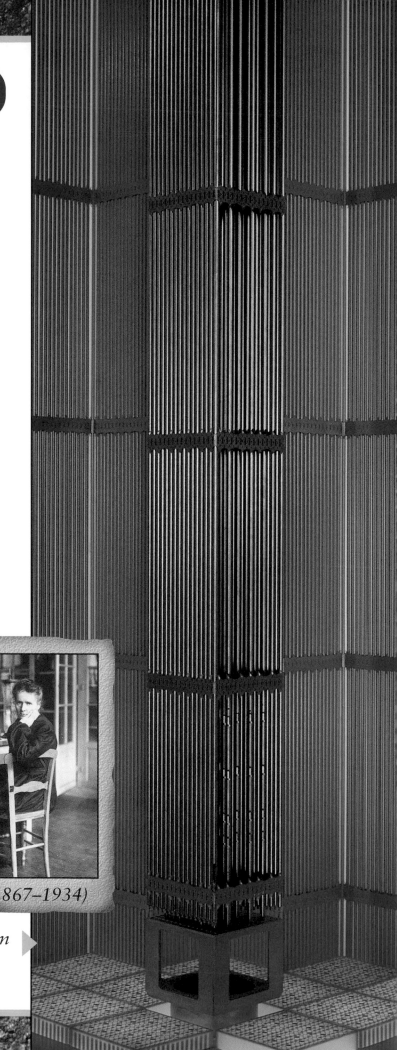

MODERN METALS

There are more than ninety known pure natural substances. These are called chemical elements. About seventy of these are metals. Many new discoveries in science and technology rely on rare metals that are unfamiliar in our daily lives.

METAL "CATS"

Every new car has a "cat." In cars, a "cat" is a catalytic convertor, which is a device in the exhaust system. Its job is to make engine fumes cleaner by changing polluting gases into cleaner substances. Car "cats" use rare metals, such as palladium, platinum, and rhodium to clean up exhaust.

FACTS FROM THE PAST

Polish-born French scientist Marie Curie did many experiments with metals. She found that some metals naturally give off rays and particles, which we now know can cause great harm. She invented a new term for this feature: radioactivity.

Marie Curie (1867–1934)

Nuclear power plants use metals such as uranium and plutonium as fuel. Nuclear weapons use the same metals in a similar way.

This diagram shows some of the metals in an alkaline electrical cell, or battery. The rechargeable batteries known as nicads are named after the two main metals they contain — nickel and cadmium.

One of the strangest metals, mercury, freezes into a solid at a very low temperature — -102°F (-39°C). At ordinary room temperature, mercury is therefore a liquid. It is used for medical thermometers.

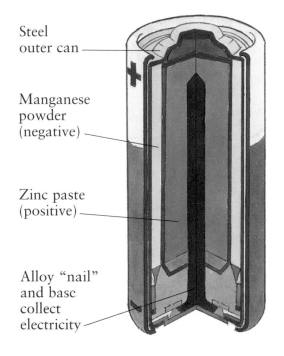

Steel outer can

Manganese powder (negative)

Zinc paste (positive)

Alloy "nail" and base collect electricity

ELECTRICITY FROM METALS

Metals such as lead, zinc, manganese, lithium, mercury, nickel, and cadmium are used in electrical batteries. They take part in the chemical processes that produce electricity. Many of these metals are harmful if they "escape" into the soil or water, however, so old batteries must be disposed of properly and with great care. Rechargeable batteries, which can be used many times, help reduce the waste and pollution caused by throwing away old batteries.

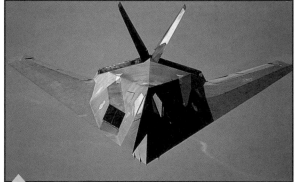

Rare metals are combined to make new alloys that are stronger, lighter, and more resistant to wear, heat, rays, and chemicals. They are used in high-tech machines such as racing cars, computers, and airplanes.

METALS IN THE FUTURE

In ancient times, people used only a few metals, such as iron, copper, lead, and tin, and their alloys, such as bronze and brass. Today we use nearly all of the metals that occur in nature — and some man-made ones that do not.

ARTIFICIAL METALS

Some metals do not occur in nature. They are artificial, or man-made, in massive "atom smasher" machines. These metals may have very specialized features, such as amazing magnetism or great radioactivity. They could be used for future research in medicine, space, computers, and other high-tech sciences.

The metal barium shows up white in X rays. People sometimes drink a "soup" of it in a medical checkup.

IDEAS FOR THE FUTURE

Supplies of metals may be limited here on Earth. But deep in space, lumps of rock called asteroids are rich in various metals, such as iron, nickel, and iridium. Now and then, one of these lumps of rock falls to Earth as a meteorite. In the future, we may send spacecrafts to mine these rocks, refine their ores, and bring their metals back to Earth.

Meteorite that landed in Texas

Scientists need fast computers to aid their research. Superconductor alloys will speed up their equipment.

Many metals can be recycled, saving raw materials, time, natural habitats, and energy. Recycling also prevents waste and pollution. Recyclable metals include aluminum, iron, steel, copper, lead, gold, silver, and brass. Many new products have recyclable parts built into their designs.

METAL PROBLEMS

Extracting and refining metals from their ores uses up vast amounts of chemicals and raw materials. It also uses lots of heat and other forms of energy. This energy comes mostly from coal, oil, and gas — fuels that will soon be in short supply if we continue to use them so fast. Also, strip mines scar the land, and giant piles of leftover rocks cause huge problems of waste and pollution.

SAVING METALS

In addition, we have already used much of the ore that is richest in metals. In the future, we will have to process more ore to extract less metal. These are just some of the reasons that saving and recycling metals are so important.

Will we mine asteroids in space?

29

METALS AND THEIR USES

	TYPE OF METAL	FEATURES AND USES
INDUSTRIAL METALS	Iron (*chemical symbol — Fe*)	Heavy, quite strong, magnetic, can be cast and forged, but rusts in damp conditions; used for decorative metalwork, combined with other metals and carbon to make steels
	Steel (alloy of iron)	Very strong, can be made in many varieties, including stainless; used for girders, beams, frames, sheets, cars, appliances, machines, cans, nuts, bolts, tools, cutlery, many other items
	Aluminum (*Al*)	Light, strong, slightly brittle; used mainly as alloys in planes, electrical cables, lightweight parts, cans, cartons, cookware, foil
	Copper (*Cu*)	Conducts electricity well, resists corrosion; used for wires, tubes, cables, pipes, chemical containers, machine parts
	Tin (*Sn*)	Resists corrosion well; used to cover other metal items, such as steel containers ("tin" cans), by electroplating or dipping
PRECIOUS METALS	Gold (*Au*)	Very valuable, easily worked, resists corrosion; used for rings, bracelets and other kinds of jewelry, electroplating, coins, electrical equipment, heat shields, bearings, medicine
	Silver (*Ag*)	Valuable, easily worked, resists corrosion; used for rings and other jewelry, electroplating, coins, electrical equipment
	Platinum (*Pt*)	Very tough and durable; used for bearings, machine parts, jewelry, and scientific equipment
OTHER METALS	Mercury (*Hg*)	Silvery liquid at normal temperature; used in batteries, electrical equipment, chemicals, thermometers, dentistry
	Cadmium (*Cd*)	Fairly soft and silvery, similar to zinc; used for electroplating, and for alloys that melt at low temperatures (as in fire alarms)
	Nickel (*Ni*)	Hard, silvery-white; used in alloys, and for electroplating other items, chemical reactions, supermagnets
	Chromium (*Cr*)	Extremely hard, tough, and shiny; used for electroplating other items, and in making bearings, moving parts, and stainless steel
	Ytterbium (*Yb*)	Rare, silvery; almost no important uses

GLOSSARY

alloy: a metal made of a certain metal and one or more other substances.

carbon: a black element that makes up soot and is used in alloys.

conductor: a substance that carries electricity (electrical conductor) or heat (thermal conductor) very well. Most metals do both.

corrosion: the process of wearing away, especially when attacked by chemicals.

extract: to remove metal from ore by such processes as heating (smelting), pressure, and treating with chemicals.

minerals: natural, usually crystalline, substances that are not living. Rocks are made of minerals.

ore: a rock or similar substance in the ground that is dug up so the metal in it can be extracted.

radioactivity: invisible rays and particles given off (radiated) by certain substances. These rays may harm living things, but they are also used to treat diseases such as cancer.

refining: making a metal more pure by removing other substances from it.

slag: waste material left over from the refining process.

solder: an alloy that can be melted and used to join metal parts together.

MORE BOOKS TO READ

Aluminum. The Elements series. John Farndon (Marshall Cavendish Corporation)

Gold. The Elements series. Sarah Angliss (Marshall Cavendish Corporation)

How Steel Is Made. I Wonder series. Neil Curtis, Peter Greenland (Lerner Publications Company)

Iron. The Elements series. Giles Sparrow (Marshall Cavendish Corporation)

WEB SITES

A Wonderful World of Minerals — Metals. http://library.thinkquest.org/J002744/adlm-mtls.html?tqskip=1

Industrial Revolution — Metallurgy http://www.woodberry.org/acad/hist/irwww/Metallurgy/index.htm

Due to the dynamic nature of the Internet, some web sites stay current longer than others. To find additional web sites, use a reliable search engine with one or more of the following keywords: *alloys, aluminum, copper, Marie Curie, electroplating, gold, iron, metal, mining, silver, smelting, steel.*

INDEX